MINDSET
RE-MINDER

365 Days of Inspiring Quotes and Contemplations to Discover Your Inner Strength and Transform Your Life from the Inside Out

BETH BIANCA

Blue PLUTO Publishing

"MINDSET RE-MINDER: 365 Days of Inspiring Quotes and Contemplations to Discover Your Inner Strength and Transform Your Life from the Inside Out"

Mindset Re-Minder: 365 Days of Inspiring Quotes and Contemplations to Discover Your Inner Strength and Transform Your Life from the Inside Out / Beth Bianca – 1st ed.

ISBN-13: 978-0-692-99701-7

Also by Beth Bianca:

Mindset Breakthrough: *Achieve Weight-Loss Surgery Success*
The Breakthrough Journal: *Butterfly Edition*
The Breakthrough Journal: *Flower Edition*

Join Beth's motivational community, using your phone.
Text **LIVING** to **444999**

Learn more at: **BethBianca.com**

ACKNOWLEDGEMENTS

I am thankful to God for giving me a second chance to live, learn, and share.

To my peeps, Carlene, Lydia, Gina, and Robin. Thank you for your continued support. Without your help, this book would not have been possible.

INTRODUCTION

In today's busy world it's easy to get distracted from what's important. Most people know what they should be doing, but they don't have the follow-through to get it done.

The Mindset Re-Minder is here to help you stay focused on what matters most. It will work with you to unveil your inner strength through 365 inspiring quotes with commentary that will change your world from the inside out. It's a daily motivational reminder to do what needs to be done to become the person you're meant to Be.

As an author of four books, a bariatric patient who lost 229 pounds, and a certified life coach, I discovered the keys to success are found in our daily routines. When you conquer your habits, achieving success becomes inevitable.

Each inspiring quote was hand-picked based on its

relevance for creating positive changes in your life. The same principles that have worked for centuries are still applicable today. There is no magic secret to achieving success. What has worked for so many others will work for you too.

If you read and apply the knowledge found in the pages of this book, every day, your life will be positively changed.

Don't be the person who keeps waiting for someday to arrive. Be the person who makes things happen. Be the person that others admire because you do what needs to be done to achieve success. Be the person who takes action immediately and pursues their dreams without reservations.

Make every day matter with the Mindset Re-Minder. Start reading it today.

BEFORE YOU START

This is more than a compilation of quotes. It's a path to learning the principles of success.

Each quote shares a principle that you can apply to your everyday life. Read and re-read the quotes on a daily basis and mark the entries that resonate with you. Then you can return to review them when you need a gentle nudge, in the right direction.

Repetition is the key to learning. The more a message is repeated, the faster your mind will accept it. It's similar to how advertising works. Companies pay big money for repeatedly presenting their messages to you.

This book will serve as a method for laying a foundation for success in your life. The fundamentals are repeated through 365 different quotes and contemplations. You'll be training your subconscious mind, by simply reading the quotes from the various viewpoints. This will allow you to learn the principals of success with little effort. All you need to do is read the quotes and apply what you learn.

I hope you find this book helpful and inspirational, during your journey, of becoming who you're meant to Be.

DAY 1

If you want to be happy,
set a goal that commands your thoughts,
liberates your energy and inspires your hopes.
~Andrew Carnegie

When setting a goal, it must be something that inspires you to take action. If it's not something you're dreaming to see in your life, you will not have the determination to achieve it.

DAY 2

The greatest weapon against stress is our ability
to choose one thought over another.
~William James

What you think about grows.
Choose thoughts that empower you
to live life, not suffer from
the circumstances.

DAY 3

Don't let what you cannot do interfere with what you can do.
~John R. Wooden

It's easy to think we can't do anything if we can't do everything. There is always something we can do. Find what works for you and then just do it.

DAY 4

The whole life of man is but a point of time, let us enjoy it, therefore, while it lasts, and not spend it to no purpose.
~Plutarch

It's easy to live like we have an infinite number of days, in front of us. When we do that, we're losing today and what we could Be tomorrow.

DAY 5

Never condemn yourself.
Always affirm positive words into your life.
~Lailah Gifty Akita

The world already has too much negativity.
Don't add your voice to the noise. Build
yourself up with positive self-talk and take
on any challenges with strength.

DAY 6

We are the products of our past,
but we don't have to be prisoners of it.
~Rick Warren

Break free from your past.
Today is a new day to begin building
your better tomorrows.

DAY 7

*Repetition of the same thought or physical action
develops into a habit which, repeated frequently
enough, becomes an automatic reflex.*
~Norman Vincent Peale

Daily, repeated, and consistent
behaviors create our habits.

The best way to succeed in
reaching our goals is to create
new empowering habits.

Do what you know you should be
doing. And, keep doing that until it
becomes part of your regular routine.

Positive habits create a brighter
future. Negative habits keep
you bound to your past.

Create habits that bring you
closer to your goals, not farther
away from them.

DAY 8

Sight is seeing with the eyes; vision is seeing with the mind.
~Orrin Woodward

If nothing were impossible, how would your perfect life be? Write it out, visualize it, and read it over and over. The more excited you become about your future, the less likely you are to go off course.

DAY 9

Have patience. All things are difficult before they become easy.
~Saadi

Most things are not easy to do in the beginning. However, the more we apply ourselves, the easier it becomes. Don't quit. A new positive behavior will transform your life.

DAY 10

When I let go of what I am, I become what I might Be.
~Lao Tzu

The tighter we hold on to our past, the longer we stay the same. Only by letting go of those regrets, sorrows, and behaviors do we give ourselves the freedom to become something more.

DAY 11

Success must be felt inside before it can be seen on the outside.
~Author Unknown

Creating success in your life is an inside job. Trying to change your circumstances without changing your mindset is like shuffling your problems around. Permanent results come from changing your thoughts, feelings, and actions first.

DAY 12

There is a difference between interest and commitment. When you are interested in doing something you do it only when it's convenient. When you are committed to do something you accept no excuses, only results.
~Ken Blanchard

Success in life requires commitment. When something is important, you do what's necessary. No excuses, only results.

DAY 13

Sometimes great achievements arrive much later than we expect, but they arrive, and they are great.
~Sira Masetti

Patience and perseverance walk hand in hand with us on our journey. Don't question your ability to achieve your goal. Believe that success is already yours in your heart. That's when you'll see great things begin to happen in your life.

DAY 14

Nurture your mind with great thoughts,
for you will never go any higher than you think.
~Benjamin Disraeli

Think thoughts of confidence and
success. What we believe about
ourselves becomes our reality.

If we question how far we can go
toward achieving our goals, we've
already put doubt into our minds.

Believe in yourself. Know that you can
Be and Do whatever you choose.

Give yourself permission to reach
high and far with confidence.

DAY 15

The great thing in this world is not so much where we stand, as in what direction we are moving.
~Oliver Wendell Holmes Sr.

Are you heading in the direction of your goals? Your choices and actions determine your direction. And, they are thankfully both within your control.

DAY 16

Optimism is the faith that leads to achievement. Nothing can be done without hope and confidence.
~Helen Keller

Optimism is the nourishment required to achieve our goals. It keeps our focus on the rewards, instead of the struggles.

DAY 17

If one asks for success and prepares for failure,
one will get the situation one has prepared for.
~Florence Scovel

Prepare yourself for success, think success, visualize success, and act as if you are a success. There is no room for negativity or fear when all your energy is focused toward success.

DAY 18

To be responsible, keep your promises to others.
To be successful, keep your promises to yourself.
~Marie Forleo

When you care about yourself as much as you do for others, you will see incredible changes in your life. You are worthy of keeping your own promises.

DAY 19

The first step toward success is taken when you refuse to be a captive of the environment in which you first find yourself.
~Mark Caine

Don't be captive to your current circumstances. Set yourself FREE from negative thoughts and behaviors. There is much more "life' waiting for you to experience.

DAY 20

Though no one can go back and make a brand new start, anyone can start from now and make a brand new ending.
~Carl Bard

Don't let your past stand in the way of your future. When you embrace the past, you lose hope for the future. Embrace today and create a magnificent future.

DAY 21

Courage doesn't happen when you have all the answers.
It happens when you are ready to face the questions
you have been avoiding your whole life.
~Shannon L. Alder

Just because things have been a certain way your whole life, doesn't mean they have to stay that way.

You have the power to change.

It's a law of nature to change.

There is the day followed by night.
There is spring, summer,
fall, and winter.
The caterpillar transforms
into a butterfly.

Nature is always changing and
so can you.

DAY 22

Be who you set out to be.
~Gino Norris

Every day gives us a new opportunity to change. You don't have to settle for less. Become everything you are meant to Be.

DAY 23

Belief in limitation is the one and only thing that causes limitation.
~Thomas Troward

Success is available to everyone. Expand your vision and reach farther than you thought possible. Believing that you can achieve your goal is the surest way of accomplishing it.

DAY 24

If you choose to take control, you will be in charge.
~Shad Helmstetter, Ph.D.

Until you decide to "take control" of your life, you have no idea how powerful you truly are. Don't let "life" happen to you; create the life you want to live.

DAY 25

We run carelessly to the precipice after we have put something before us to prevent us seeing it.
~Blaise Pascal

When we lose focus of our destination, we end up straying from our path. Don't let anything block your view; you'll end up falling back to where you began.

DAY 26

Success and failure are not overnight experiences;
it's all the small decisions along the way
that cause people to fail or succeed.
~Tony Robbins

Every choice we make has consequences.
Good or bad, it always comes back
to our decisions. Choose wisely.

DAY 27

Gratitude is not just a word; it is a way of life.
~Rob Martin

Being grateful for what you have right
now gives you more to be thankful for
tomorrow. Don't wait to be happy with
your life, be grateful for today.

DAY 28

*Never say anything about yourself
you do not want to come true.*
~Brian Tracy

Our self-talk and the way we describe
ourselves to others is important.

These statements become our
personal affirmations. The more
we use them, the more significant
their influence is in our lives.

What we say about ourselves
will become our reality. And,
it happens whether we
realize that or not.

DAY 29

Successful people are not gifted;
they just work hard, then succeed on purpose.
~G.K. Nielson

Success doesn't happen by accident.
It starts with having a purpose
then taking action every day until
that purpose becomes a reality. We will
succeed because there is a purpose.

DAY 30

At the center of your being you have the answer;
You know who you are and you know what you want.
~Lao Tzu.

Years of outside conditioning builds a wall that
prevents us from seeing, who we're meant to Be.
Dig deep and rediscover your authentic self.
Then begin to create the life you want to live.

DAY 31

Every next level of your life will demand a different you.
~Leonardo DiCaprio

The only way to achieve more in our lives is by becoming more ourselves. The changes we make within us affect the changes we see in our lives—good, bad, or the same. It all begins with our mindset.

DAY 32

Create the life you can't wait to wake up to.
~Josie Spinardi

Your life is created by the choices you make. You can create something amazing. Or, you can choose to do nothing and live in the wake of other people's choices for you. Choose amazing for yourself.

Feb 2

DAY 33

You have to dream before your dreams can come true.
~A. P. J. Abdul Kalam

Before you can get where you are going, you need to know, where to go. Write your goal down in vivid detail. Then, there'll be no mistake to where you're heading.

DAY 34

Obstacles are things a person sees when he takes his eyes off his goal.
~E. Joseph Cossman

There are ups and downs on every journey. But, when you stay focused on the vision of your goal being achieved, nothing will keep you from reaching it.

DAY 35

Patience is not simply the ability to wait—
It's how we behave while we're waiting.
~Joyce Meyer

Almost everyone knows that patience is required while reaching our goals.

However, most of us are not fans of waiting. We want everything, and we want it right now.

But, have you given any thought to how our behavior, while we "wait," affects the results we eventually do see in our lives?

Don't let the time it takes to reach your goals discourage you. That will only cause a bigger delay. Always keep moving forward. That's the only way to reach your destination.

215

DAY 36

*A flower does not think of competing with the flower next to it.
It just blooms.*
~Zen Shin

Comparing ourselves to others takes away the joy of our own progress. Everyone's journey is different. Appreciate where you are today and be thankful for how far you've already come.

216

DAY 37

Dream lofty dreams, and as you dream, so shall you become.
~James Allen

You have the potential to become everything you desire. Dream a big dream and then take all the steps to reach it.

DAY 38

A person is what he thinks about all day long.
~Ralph Waldo Emerson

Pay attention to the way you think and talk about yourself. Would you let anyone else speak to you that way? Be your biggest cheerleader, instead of your harshest critic.

DAY 39

Your past is just a story.
And once you realize this, it has no power over you.
~Chuck Palahniuk

Every moment is another opportunity to change. Don't worry about yesterday. Right now, you have the power to change today.

DAY 40

If you want something you never had,
you have to do something you've never done.
~Thomas Jefferson

Change begins with you. When you change your thoughts and actions, you'll start to see different results in your life.

DAY 41

Don't let your habits become handcuffs.
~Elizabeth Berg

What we consistently and repeatedly do will become a habit. Don't hold on to habits that limit you. Instead, choose to create habits that bring you the freedom to LIVE life.

DAY 42

Visualize this thing that you want,
see it, feel it, believe in it.
Make your mental blue print,
and begin to build.
~Robert Collier

It is easier to make changes in our lives when we use the power of our subconscious mind.

Your subconscious guides you to whatever you think about the most. And, it doesn't matter whether you're thinking of something good or bad.

Let your subconscious know what is important to you. Focus on your goal with vivid detail and emotion.

Then soon enough, you'll find your actions guiding you toward your vision, instead of fighting against you.

DAY 43

The journey in between what you once were and who you are now becoming is where the dance of life takes place.
~Barbara De Angelis

Value your journey as much as your goal. That's where we become the person we're meant to be. That's where the real changes happen.

DAY 44

Turn your face to the sun and the shadows fall behind you.
~Maori Proverb

Staying positive isn't always easy. But, being negative isn't easy either. Look for the bright side in every situation.

DAY 45

Success is like a snowball, it takes momentum to build.
~Steve Ferrante

We reach our goals by taking small actions every day. Don't look for perfection, look for consistent progress and continue to build.

DAY 46

Don't let your struggle become your identity.
~Ralston Bowles

Sometimes the stress in our lives can seem overwhelming. Don't let what's happening to you become who you are. The events in your life do not define you. You define yourself.

2/16

DAY 47

We are the start and end point of every transformation.
~Joseph Rain

Transformation begins the moment you decide to change. It is achieved by taking immediate action and never quitting until your goal is a reality.

2/17

DAY 48

Trust the process. Your time is coming.
Just do the work, the results will handle themselves.
~Tony Gaskins

Do you doubt that the sun will rise in the morning? Then don't doubt your success either. You will see results for the work you do. Just like the sun rises every morning—it's a law of nature.

DAY 49

It is in your moments of decision that your destiny is shaped.
~Tony Robbins

We make decisions all day long.
Should I do this, should I do that?
I don't feel like doing this . . .

Every decision matters.

It's not always a big decision
that changes our lives.

Most of the time, it's all the small
decisions we make along the way,
that change us even more.

2/19

DAY 50

The question isn't who's going to let me;
it's who's going to stop me.
~Ayn Rand

Be so determined in your decisions
that nothing will stop you from
reaching your goals.

2/20

DAY 51

The most common way people give up their power
is by thinking they don't have any.
~Alice Walker

You have the power to change your life.
When you take responsibility for your
thoughts and behaviors, you take control
of your results. It's powerful to know that
reaching your goal is inevitable.

DAY 52

*What you get by achieving your goals is not as important
as what you become by achieving your goals.*
~Henry David Thoreau

Achieving our goals is a worthy endeavor.
But, the person we become to create that
success is what changes our lives forever.

DAY 53

*Every time you are tempted to react in the same old way,
ask if you want to be a prisoner of the past
or a pioneer of the future.*
~Deepak Chopra

Break free from your old behaviors. Don't
be a victim of your past. Instead, be a
trailblazer to your new future.

DAY 54

It's not that we have little time,
but more that we waste a good deal of it.
~Seneca

Every indulgence, every avoidance, every detour
wastes our precious time. Days, weeks, months,
and years pass, while pieces of our life slip away.
Today, you can become the force of change.
Create something new for yourself.

DAY 55

It all begins and ends in your mind. What you give
power to has power over you, if you allow it.
~Leon Brown

Are you in control of your thoughts? If negative
thinking grows in your mind, you are giving your
power away. Instead, choose positive thoughts
that empower you to achieve your goals.

DAY 56

Strength doesn't come from what you can do. It comes from overcoming the things you once thought you couldn't.
~Rikki Rogers

Achieving our goals can be difficult at times.

If it were something that could be accomplished with little effort, there would be no reason to set a goal.

Just like building a muscle, we can increase our determination and perseverance. You can overcome all obstacles and challenges.

Once you know this, you'll have overcome the biggest obstacle to achieving success.

DAY 57

Make the most of yourself, for that is all there is of you.
~Ralph Waldo Emerson

It doesn't have to be complicated. Begin with small improvements every day. Start today and don't stop until you become who you want to BE.

DAY 58

The grateful mind continually expects good things, and expectation becomes faith.
~Wallace D. Wattles

Being grateful for the good in your life opens the door for more good to come into your life.

DAY 59

The real winners I've met in life weren't necessarily skilled or perfect. They just had the tenacity to never, ever give up.
~Curtis Rivers

Perfection isn't required to achieve our goals. What is essential is to never, ever give up.

DAY 60

One reason people resist change is because they focus on what they have to give up, instead of what they have to gain.
~Rick Godwin

What are you focusing on while reaching your goals? Focus on the affect success will have on your life, not the work you're putting in. You'll soon discover that your effort will not have been in vain.

march 2

DAY 61

Life is unfolding by each step you take, but,
it is fulfilled by every choice you make.
~Eleesha

Our life passes before us every day. But,
it's our choices that affect the life we end
up living. What you do today matters.
Do what brings your dream to life.

march 3

DAY 62

The will is your most important asset.
If you lose it, you have lost everything.
~Dele Ayo Bankole

Always nurture your will, with a
magnificent vision of your goal
already being achieved. Feed the fire
of determination every day.

314

DAY 63

When someone criticizes you,
it defines who they are, not who you are.
~Marie Forleo

How beautiful would it be if everyone
in your life was your cheerleader?

It's too bad that's not always the case.

Don't give power to the naysayers by
dwelling on their comments. You have
more exciting things to contemplate.

Your strength comes from within.
Continue on your journey and claim
the success you deserve.

You are worthy of your heart's desires.

315

DAY 64

Change is progress, not an event.
~Beth Bianca

Change takes time. It happens through our deliberate, consistent, and positive actions. Look for progress, not perfection, and always keep moving forward.

316

DAY 65

You're only as weak as you let yourself become, and you're only as strong as you allow yourself to be.
~Daniel Hansen

Rise to your potential. You can overcome, push through, and conquer anything with your determination.

DAY 66

Life is not about waiting for the storms to pass.
It's about learning how to dance in the rain.
~Vivian Greene

There will be uncomfortable circumstances in
life. And, there will be challenges that seem
overwhelming at times. Find your inner strength
to forge ahead, no matter what happens.
You are stronger than you know.

DAY 67

You've got to get up every morning with determination
if you're going to go to bed with satisfaction.
~George Lorimer

Decide that today will be a marvelous day.
You get to determine what your day
becomes by the thoughts you think
and the actions you take.

3/9

DAY 68

*To be content does not mean that you don't desire more,
it means you're thankful for what you have
and patient for what's to come.*
~Tony Gaskins

Take a moment and notice how far you've
already come on your journey. And, be
happy today while doing what needs to
be done for tomorrow.

3/10

DAY 69

What I'm looking for is not out there, it is in me.
~Helen Keller

Everything you desire to Be is already
inside you. All you need to do is permit
yourself to see it. Everything will be
revealed when you dare to look.

3/11

DAY 70

Setting goals is the first step in turning
the invisible into the visible.
~Tony Robbins

There are two types of goals we can use to become the person we desire to BE.

First, we need a big, impressive goal— one that is so exciting it fuels us to do what needs to be done.

Secondly, we need smaller goals on the way to our big goal. They're the stepping stones we use to reach our impressive goal. Small goals are achieved quickly and help to keep us encouraged during our journey.

Use both types of goals to make every day count on your way to success.

3/12

DAY 71

I am not concerned that you have fallen.
I am concerned that you arise.
~Abraham Lincoln

We all trip and make mistakes.
What's important is that we recover
quickly. Don't wait: get back up.
Always keep moving forward.

3/13

DAY 72

Doubting your ability to get what you long for
is like trying to reach east by traveling west.
~Baudouin

We must believe that we can achieve our
goals. That belief ignites the desire
to push through all adversity.

3\14

DAY 73

Willpower is the art of replacing one habit for another.
~Michael Garofalo

The key to breaking a negative habit is to replace it with a new positive habit. Don't fight the old habit. Put all of your efforts into building the new habit.

3\15

DAY 74

Self-talk reflects your innermost feelings.
~Asa Don Brown, Ph.D.

What are you telling yourself? Are you building yourself up to succeed or tearing yourself down to fail? Always build yourself up with positive self-talk.

3/16

DAY 75

Successful people realize their journey is unique and can't be compared. So don't get stuck in the comparison trap–stay focused on your why.
~Jim Rohn

No good comes from comparing ourselves to others. All that matters is that you are farther ahead today than where you were yesterday.

3/17

DAY 76

If you are going to achieve excellence in big things, you develop the habit in little matters.
~Colin Powell

Small consistent steps bring us to our success. Create the habit of completing all the right activities every day. You'll get there faster.

3/18

DAY 77

You were designed, from birth, to succeed.
~Shad Helmstetter, Ph.D.

We are all born with unlimited potential.

Although, at some point, we let life's problems tear us down, instead of using the challenges to build our strengths.

Go back and open the tap to your enthusiasm. Live your life with the child-like spirit of adventure again.

Get that sparkle back in your eyes.

You are destined for success!

3/19

DAY 78

*The beautiful journey of today can only begin
when we learn to let go of yesterday.*
~Steve Maraboli

Today is a new day with new
opportunities. Create your beautiful
journey ahead and stop looking behind.
Move forward with confidence.

3/20

DAY 79

Stop seeking out the storms and enjoy more fully the sunlight.
~Gordon B. Hinckley

Don't let negative thoughts get in the way
of your happiness. Accept the good in
your life. Accept the person you are.
Embrace your success completely.

3/21

DAY 80

To conquer frustration, one must remain intensely focused on the outcome, not the obstacles.
~T.F. Hodge

When we run into obstacles on our journey, it can be frustrating. Don't let those unplanned issues stop you from reaching your goals. Stay focused on the reward. Your determination will bring you success.

3/22

DAY 81

I will find new habits, new thoughts, new rules. I will become something else.
~Veronica Roth

Whether we are becoming more or something less is determined by our thoughts, feelings, and actions. Don't go with the flow of events, choose your thoughts and actions with purpose. Then you'll be in control of who you become.

3/23

DAY 82

*Stop being who you think you should be
and start being who you truly are.*
~Cara Leyba

Sometimes we get caught up with what
others expect from us, and we forget
who we really are. Claim your life back
and BE yourself.

3/24

DAY 83

First we make our habits, then our habits make us.
~John Dryden

Habits are habits;
we determine if they are good or bad. But,
choose your habits wisely because they will
determine who you become.

3/25

DAY 84

*The difference between who you are and
who you want to be is what you do.*
~Bill Phillips

Success comes from taking consistent
positive actions every day.

Do you know what you should be doing?

If not, find out and then start doing it.

Knowing what to do and then doing it
is the difference between those who
succeed and those who do not.

Do the thing you know
you should be doing.

DAY 85

When we make positive choices, we are not depriving ourselves.
We are creating ourselves.
~Beth Bianca

Don't let feelings of deprivation prevent you from making choices that bring you closer to your goal. Those decisions bring you the life you long to live.

DAY 86

Wherever you go, go with all your heart.
~Confucius

When you want something with all of your heart, you will find a way to achieve it. Put your heart into everything you do.

DAY 87

*A river cuts through rock not because of its power,
but because of its persistence.*
~James N. Watkins

Persistence gets us through the obstacles and
challenges we face. Persistence helps us to
create new positive habits. Persistence is the
difference between success and failure.

DAY 88

To know and not to do is really not to know.
~Stephen R. Covey

It doesn't matter how much you know.
All knowledge has value when it's
applied in your life. Create change
by using what you learn.

3|30

DAY 89

Don't be pushed by your problems. Be led by your dreams.
~Ralph Waldo Emerson

Where you focus is where you go. Let your dreams be your guide. Leave your problems behind; they'll only take you back to where you already were.

3|31

DAY 90

Some people want it to happen. Some people wish it would happen. Some people make it happen.
~Michael Jordan

You can control your thoughts, feelings, and actions. So, Be the person who makes "it" happen.

DAY 91

Break your bad labels instead of living in them.
~Orrin Woodward

The labels we use to describe
ourselves are usually man-made
terms to explain a behavior.

Behaviors can be changed.

Don't hold on to labels that
take away your ability to choose
a better and brighter future.

You are not a label. You are an
individual capable of changing
yourself and your entire life.

Be a label breaker, not a label maker.

4/2

DAY 92

Start where you are. Use what you have. Do what you can.
~Arthur Ashe

Don't wait for a perfect time to change.
Now is always the best time to begin.

4/3

DAY 93

*Only you can take inner freedom away from yourself,
or give it to yourself. Nobody else can.*
~Michael A. Singer

It's easy to blame circumstances for not being
where we want to be. But, that's giving our
freedom away. Instead, claim responsibility,
and take your freedom back.

DAY 94

*Think big thoughts that give you strength
and make you resilient.*
~Jerry Bruckner

Think strong, powerful thoughts of success.
Don't think about failure and weakness.
What you nurture grows. Make sure it's
something you want to see more of
in your life.

DAY 95

*Having a dream is what keeps you alive. Overcoming the
challenges makes life worth living.*
~Mary Tyler Moore

Always have a big dream in your life. And,
keep working on the dream until it becomes
your reality. What happens between the dream
and its reality is the spice of life.

DAY 96

When you know what's important,
it's a lot easier to ignore what's not.
~Marie Forleo

Guard your time like a precious jewel.
Don't let everyone else's priorities become
yours. Without your time, you have nothing.

DAY 97

Procrastination is cured by taking action.
~Author Unknown

Procrastination can be a real pain. But,
it's a pain that can be easily cured.
Just do what needs to be done.
Your relief will be extraordinary.

DAY 98

Don't judge each day by the harvest you reap
but by the seeds you plant.
~Robert Louis Stevenson

The seeds we plant are the actions we
complete each day toward our goal.

The harvest we reap is our achieved
goal and the person we become
during that process.

Concentrate on doing what needs
to be done every day and you
will achieve your goal.

It really is that simple.

DAY 99

When she transformed into a butterfly, the caterpillars spoke not of her beauty, but of her weirdness. They wanted her to change back into what she always had been. But she had wings.
~Dean Jackson

Your journey is your own. Don't let any caterpillars hold you back. You're the beautiful butterfly; expand your wings and soar to new heights.

DAY 100

Man can only receive what he sees himself receiving.
~Florence Scovel Shinn

Do you see yourself achieving your goal? Once you believe that you can have success, the path for achieving it will open right in front of you.

DAY 101

Life is really simple, but we insist on making it complicated.
~Confucius

An overwhelmed mind brings life to a standstill. Stick to the fundamentals and keep things simple to accomplish. The easier you make it for yourself, the more you'll achieve.

DAY 102

Reach high, for the stars lie hidden in you.
Dream deep, for every dream precedes the goal.
~Rabindranath Tagore

Your potential is more significant than you think. Reach out and dream a big dream to see for yourself.

DAY 103

You cannot change your destination overnight,
but you can change your direction overnight.
~Jim Rohn

Making a course correction is easy. What's
important is to realize when a correction is
needed and then following through with
the appropriate actions.

DAY 104

Every bit of you is worthy of your loving.
~Pat Rodegast

Be kind to yourself. Be encouraging to
yourself. And, most of all, love yourself
as much as you love the important
people in your life.

DAY 105

*The ultimate measure of a man is not where he stands
in moments of comfort, but where he stands
at times of challenge and controversy.*
~Martin Luther King, Jr.

When our lives are calm,
it's easy to stay positive and upbeat.

But, when challenges, distractions,
and obstacles get in the way,
we often become discouraged.

Yet, these are the times that
shape us into the person who will
ultimately achieve success. Learn
from the obstacles and challenges.

Success becomes inevitable when
you stay on course.

DAY 106

Don't compare your beginning to someone else's middle.
~Tim Hiller

Recognize your accomplishments and be happy with your progress. It doesn't matter where others are on their journey. You're on the path meant for you.

DAY 107

It takes courage to grow up and become who you really are.
~E.E. Cummings

Almost anything worth achieving pushes us to be more than we were yesterday. Be courageous and keep moving forward.

4/18

DAY 108

If you fell down yesterday, stand up today.
~H.G. Wells

Yesterday is over and the possibilities of today await you. Strive for progress, not perfection. Decide to have an incredible day and then make it happen.

4/15

DAY 109

How we look at life affects the life we live.
~Beth Bianca

Our perceptions color the world we see. Change your perceptions and you'll change your world.

4/20

DAY 110

I'm the cover of a book, whose pages are still being written.
~Richard L. Ratliff

Each day is a blank page in the book of your life, and you are the author. You decide what kind of story you live. Is it an adventure, drama, comedy, or a tragedy?

4/21

DAY 111

Be positive, be happy and be thankful.
~Lailah Gifty Akita

Don't let the circumstances of your life dictate your feelings. Change the way you feel about the circumstances and you'll gain control over them.

71

DAY 112

People who succeed have momentum.
The more they succeed, the more they want
to succeed, and the more they find a way to succeed.
Similarly, when someone is failing, the tendency
is to get on a downward spiral that can even
become a self-filling prophecy.
~Tony Robbins

Use momentum to build your success,
not a downward spiral.

If you feel overwhelmed, start with
something small that's easy to
accomplish. Then, build on those
accomplishments every day.

That's how momentum
builds your confidence.
That's how momentum
helps you reach your goals.

DAY 113

The rewards of tomorrow are safely hidden in the belief of never quitting and not giving up on yourself today.
~Johnnie Dent Jr.

If you don't see the results you want, adjust your course, but stay focused on your destination. That's the one thing that shouldn't ever change. Always keep moving forward to your goal.

DAY 114

Learn from yesterday, live for today, hope for tomorrow.
~Albert Einstein

Use what you learned yesterday to make today worth living. And, always stay focused on your goal. That's what brings the hope for tomorrow.

DAY 115

If you have discipline, drive and determination,
nothing is impossible.
~Dana Linn Bailey

Put your mind, body, and spirit into
achieving your dream. When you do,
nothing will keep you from success.

DAY 116

I'm not telling you it's going to be easy.
I'm telling you it's going to be worth it.
~Art Williams

Every journey has its highs and lows. But,
when we stay determined to keep moving
forward, our rewards will be exceptional.

DAY 117

When someone tells me "no," it doesn't mean I can't do it,
it simply means I can't do it with them.
~Karen E. Quinones Miller

Don't let naysayers stand in your way.
Just go around them. There are more
important things to do. Success is
waiting for you ahead.

DAY 118

A big part of willpower is having something to aspire to,
something to live for.
~Mark Shuttleworth

Having a big "why" empowers you to do
what needs to be done to achieve success.
If you feel deprived, you better find
a bigger why.

DAY 119

The difficulty lies not so much in developing
new ideas as in escaping the old ones.
~John Maynard Keynes

Most people know what to do,
but some of us have a hard time
doing what we know.

There is no magic formula
to achieve success.

Only you have the power to escape the
old ideas that have held you captive.

Stop having defeating thoughts.
Instead, think empowering thoughts.

Small daily actions create new routines.
Move forward and build your dreams
into reality.

4/30

DAY 120

Rule your mind or it will rule you.
~Horace

Our mind can be our biggest ally or our worst foe. Pay attention to your negative thoughts, feelings, and actions. Unless you decide to control them, they will follow wherever you go.

DAY 121

Habit is persistence in practice.
~Octavia E. Butler

We are defined by our consistent and repeated actions. Choose positive, healthy actions. Then, persistently continue with those efforts until they become your new habits. You'll be creating a superhighway directly to your goal.

DAY 122

*To quit is to fail—as long as you are still
in the game you are succeeding!*
~Lindsey Rietzsch

Success is created by those who never
quit. It doesn't matter what happened
yesterday or last month. Take charge
and forge ahead today.

DAY 123

*The only person you are destined to become
is the person you decide to be.*
~Ralph Waldo Emerson

When you wake up every morning, tell
yourself who you've decided to BE.
Then, live your day with the actions
of who you choose to BE.

DAY 124

*What do I mean by concentration?
I mean focusing totally on the business at hand
and commanding your body to do exactly what you want it to do.*
~Arnold Palmer

An essential ingredient for success is the discipline to tell yourself to do something and then follow through with doing it. Is there something you've been putting off?

DAY 125

*You will become as small as your controlling desire;
as great as your dominant aspiration.*
~James Allen

Stay focused on your goal. When you fill your mind with what you truly desire, there's no room for pesky impulse choices to get in your way.

DAY 126

You cannot control what happens to you, but you can control your attitude toward what happens to you, and in that, you will be mastering change rather than allowing it to master you.
~Brian Tracy

Change is inevitable.
We can be a victim of circumstances, or we can control our thoughts, feelings, and actions toward the circumstances.

Don't let regrets, sadness, or stress rule your days. That only hinders you from advancing toward your dream.

Take control and stay on course.

Don't fight freedom.

Choose freedom!

DAY 127

Success doesn't come to you, you go to it.
~Marva Collins

Sometimes people expect success to arrive in their lives before they are willing to take any action toward it. That's not how nature works. First, you put in the effort and then you receive success as your reward.

DAY 128

You measure the size of the accomplishment by the obstacles you had to overcome to reach your goals.
~Booker T. Washington

There are going to be obstacles and challenges in our lives. That's just the way life is. But, that's why it's so life-changing when we reach our goals. If it were easy, it wouldn't mean as much.

DAY 129

*When you know what you want, and want it bad enough,
you will find a way to get it.*
~Jim Rohn

If you're having trouble sticking with your plans,
it's because your subconscious doesn't know they
are important to you. Use affirmations to train
your brain to see the importance of your goals.
Then, your mind will work with you to accomplish
your goals, instead of against you.

DAY 130

*The real key is to live in an environment where the mind feels
free to choose the right thing instead of being compelled by habit
and inertia to choose the wrong thing.*
~Deepak Chopra

Set yourself up for success. Clear your
environment of distractions and temptations.
Then, you won't be a prisoner to old
behaviors.

DAY 131

Confidence isn't optimism or pessimism, and it's not a character attribute. It's the expectation of a positive outcome.
~Rosabeth Moss Kanter

Expecting a positive outcome gives us confidence. Don't just try to do something, conquer it.

DAY 132

We are only failures in life when we give up and stop trying. If you fail, get up and try again.
~Lailah Gifty Akita

Look at "failures" as learning experiences. You just learned what doesn't work. Now, pick yourself up and keep moving ahead with your new knowledge.

DAY 133

Success is a state of mind. If you want success,
start thinking of yourself as a success.
~Dr. Joyce Brothers

Sounds simple, doesn't it? Then why is it so hard for people to achieve success?

If you are happy with your results, you're on the right course. If you're not happy, it's time to make a change.

Start visualizing yourself as a success. Don't focus on your shortcomings. Instead, focus on who you want to be, do, and have in your life.

If it doesn't feel comfortable in the beginning, just keep doing it. Keep visualizing until your vision becomes natural for you. That's when you'll start to see significant changes in your life.

DAY 134

The pain you feel today is the strength you feel tomorrow.
~Stephen Richards

Don't let the pain you feel today change your focus from reaching your goals. When you stay in control of your thoughts and behaviors, you'll build strength to overcome the obstacles.

DAY 135

Peak performers are people who approach any set of circumstances with the attitude that they can get it to turn out the way they want it to. Not once in a while. Regularly. They can count on themselves.
~Charles Garfield

Be the person who can count on themselves. Become the person who creates success regularly for the long term.

DAY 136

You can't just wish change; you have to live the change in order for it to become a reality.
~Steve Maraboli

We don't reach our goals by hoping and wishing. The journey takes effort. But, if you do the work, you will reap the rewards.

137

Practically the whole human race is hypnotized because it thinks what somebody else told it to think.
~Earnest Holmes

Do you have a "thought" that is not serving you well? Is it your own or was it planted by someone else? Replace that thought, with the completely opposite thought. Then, keep repeating the new thought until it eradicates the old one.

DAY 138

*Most of the shadows of this life are caused by
standing in one's own sunshine.*
~Ralph Waldo Emerson

Give yourself permission to live your life.
Find the freedom that's waiting
for you in the sunshine.

DAY 139

*He who is not contented with what he has, would not be
contented with what he would like to have.*
~Socrates

Being grateful for what you have improves
your life. Don't get so caught up in your
daily activity that you forget the beauty that
is already present in your life.

DAY 140

I've come to believe that all my past failure and frustrations were actually laying the foundation for the understandings that have created the new level of living I now enjoy.
~Tony Robbins

Have patience with your journey.
Don't look for the easy way out.
There are none.

Do the necessary work, because it has
to be done. The work changes you
into the person you're meant to be.

You may not understand everything at
this moment in time, but you will reach
a point when you'll know, without a
doubt, that it had a purpose.

DAY 141

*One comes to believe whatever one repeats to oneself sufficiently
often, whether the statement be true or false.*
~Robert Collier

What are you consistently repeating to yourself?
If it's not positive, it's holding you back from
your potential. Don't put obstacles on your
path to success. Clear the hurdles
from your mind.

DAY 142

Be as you wish to seem.
~Socrates

One of the surest ways of becoming
who you want to Be is to start acting
like that person today.

DAY 143

You teach people how to treat you by what you allow, what you stop, and what you reinforce.
~Tony Gaskins

Sometimes we accept bad behavior from others as a sign of our love for them. You deserve better. Teach them how you should be treated. You are worthy of respect from those in your life.

DAY 144

Argue for your limitations and, sure enough, they're yours.
~Richard Bach

Are you fighting to protect your limitations by making excuses and blaming others? Instead, you should fight to grow your possibilities.

DAY 145

If we wait for the moment when everything,
absolutely everything, is ready, we shall never begin.
~Ivan Turgenev

The perfect time to start is right now.
Don't waste another day waiting
for everything to be perfect.
That day will never come.

DAY 146

The mind that is anxious about future events is miserable.
~Seneca

Worrying about what might happen
tomorrow takes your joy
from living today.

DAY 147

You deserve the right to own and control your own thoughts. You are your thoughts. Don't ever let anyone else have dominion over them.
~Shad Helmstetter, Ph.D.

Sometimes we forget that our thoughts are our domain.

Our thoughts determine how we see the world around us, what we choose to do or not do, and how we feel about ourselves.

Ultimately, our thoughts create the life we live and are the determining factor in our success or failure.

All of this is within your control. If you choose to do nothing with your power, you'll be controlled by others who use their power.

DAY 148

Success is the sum of small efforts repeated day in and day out.
~Robert Collier

Make success simple for yourself. Small actions repeated consistently every day have more power to change your life than one large action completed periodically.

DAY 149

You are already that which you want to Be, and your refusal to believe this is the only reason you do not see it.
~Neville Goddard

Believe that what you hope to Be is already within you. Open the door to your mind and accept all that is waiting for you.

DAY 150

Discipline simply means staying focused on chipping away at the identified tasks you need to complete in order to eventually realize your goals and achieve success.
~Jonathan Mills

Stay focused on what you need to do today to reach your goals. There will always be something that will vie for your attention. It's your decision to be distracted or stay on course.

DAY 151

Effort only fully releases its reward after a person refuses to quit.
~Napoleon Hill

It would be nice if this quote were incorrect. But, knowing it's true will prepare you for your journey. There may be times when you feel like quitting. Remember then that you are close to achieving your success.

DAY 152

*All the art of living lies in a fine mingling
of letting go and holding on.*
~Henry Ellis

Let go of your past failures, grievances,
and pain. Hold on to all that empowers
you to live your life fully.

DAY 153

*Positive thinking will let you do everything better
than negative thinking will.*
~Zig Ziglar

Positive thinking nurtures success.
Negative thinking is like a poison. It kills
whatever is in its path.

DAY 154

The least lack of discipline starts to erode our self-esteem.
~Jim Rohn

We think it's ok to skip "this" today.
We think it's ok to indulge with "that"
today. And, before you know it,
all the skipping and indulging brings
a halt to our progress.

We've lost the momentum toward
achieving our goal.

Think long and hard before allowing
old behaviors back into your life.
They do not serve you well.

DAY 155

What we dwell on is who we become.
~Oprah Winfrey

Dwell on your success for today and your tomorrows. Your thoughts are like currency. Spend them wisely.

DAY 156

We cannot really think in one way and act in another.
~Thomas Troward

When you are working toward reaching your goals, make sure that you're thinking about your success. You cannot achieve what you do not believe for yourself.

DAY 157

Don't blame; only resolve.
~Neville Goddard

Challenges and obstacles will appear during your journey. When they do, don't look for a reason to blame yourself or others. Instead, use your inner strength and resolve to conquer the circumstances.

DAY 158

No idea, no matter how good, will work if it doesn't get used.
~Shad Helmstetter, Ph.D.

Have you learned something that resonated with you, but never took the time to implement it? Everything changes when you take action. Don't let old excuses hold you back from the success you deserve. Change your behavior and you change your life.

DAY 159

With a burning ambition, sustained focus, and daily action — there simply are no limits to what you will achieve.
~Curtis Rivers

Fuel the flame of your ambition with a limitless vision, a dream so incredible that it propels you into action.

DAY 160

The only person who can pull me down is myself, and I'm not going to let myself pull me down anymore.
~C. JoyBell C.

Wherever you are on your journey, you must believe that you can achieve your goals. There is no room for negative self-talk when you're working to create your success.

DAY 161

Motivation is what gets you started.
Habit is what keeps you going.
~Jim Rohn

We all need the excitement of being motivated to start our journey toward success. But, sometimes, that initial excitement weakens. When that happens, we start using our current habits to make our daily choices.

If we've created new positive habits, we'll continue toward our goals.
If we fall back into old habits, we'll end up back where we started.

Build new positive habits for success while you're motivated and excited. Then, you won't fall back into old habits when challenges appear.

DAY 162

Sometimes we focus so much on what we don't have that we fail to see, appreciate, and use what we do have.
~Jeff Dixon

It's important to be grateful for what we have today. Sometimes we keep waiting for that magic moment to appear before we can be happy. Don't "wait" your days away.

DAY 163

Nobody made a greater mistake than he who did nothing because he could do only a little.
~Edmund Burke

Sometimes we think that we can't do anything if we can't do everything. That's limited thinking. Start doing whatever you can today. The rest will come in time.

DAY 164

Don't let the fear of the time it will take to accomplish something stand in the way of your doing it. The time will pass anyway; we might just as well put that passing time to the best possible use.
~Earl Nightingale

Don't worry about how long it will take to reach your goal. If you never start, you'll never get there.

DAY 165

People in their handlings of affairs often fail when they are about to succeed. If one remains as careful at the end as he was at the beginning, there will be no failure.
~Lao Tzu

When you become fatigued, and your actions begin to drift off course, fan the flame of your determination. It's time to refocus your captivating vision.

DAY 166

*You must expect great things of yourself
before you can do them.*
~Michael Jordan

Spend more time expecting the great
things you can do and less time worrying
about the problems holding you back.

DAY 167

*If we all did the things we are capable of,
we would literally astound ourselves.*
~Thomas Edison

Surprise yourself and everyone around
you. Do something astounding!

DAY 168

*My will shall shape the future. Whether I fail
or succeed shall be no one's doing but my own.
I am the force. I can clear any obstacle before
me or I can be lost in the maze. My choice.
My responsibility. Win or lose only I
hold the key to my destiny.*
~Elaine Maxwell

Can you feel the determination
of this quote?

Take time today and write your
statement of determination. Then
make it your daily mantra.

When you feel passion for what you're
doing, nothing will stand in the way
of achieving your dream.

Ignite the spark within you.

DAY 169

There is a tremendous difference between existing and thriving. Regardless of our age, we need the life force of joy—joie de vivre.
~Laurie Buchanan, Ph.D.

Seize the day!
Life is too short just to let the days pass.
What can you do differently today?

DAY 170

Always concentrate on how far you have come, rather than how far you have left to go. The difference in how easy it seems will amaze you.
~Heidi Johnson

No matter where you are on your journey, you are farther along than you were when you started. Give yourself credit for your success, no matter how small you think it is.

DAY 171

Your choices reflect your priorities.
~Jean A. Stevens

Don't talk about your priorities.
Instead, show the world your
priorities. The choices you make
and the actions you take every day
speak louder than any words.

DAY 172

When at last, I ceased to be myself, I came to Be.
~Kamand Kojouri

Let go of your self-defeating beliefs.
Move out of your comfort zone.
Permit yourself to experience life
on a whole new level.

DAY 173

The chief cause of failure and unhappiness is trading what we want most for what we want in the moment.
~Bertrand Russell

Remember the "why" of your goal and don't be swayed by the impulses that would move you away from it.

DAY 174

When a flower doesn't bloom you fix the environment in which it grows, not the flower.
~Alexander den Heijer

If something in your environment is hindering you from reaching your goal, find a way to fix it. You deserve to bloom, just like the flower.

DAY 175

A dream written down with a date becomes a goal.
A goal broken down into steps becomes a plan.
A plan backed by action makes your dreams come true.
~Greg S. Reid

Don't be deceived by the simplicity of this quote. It's a blueprint for success.

If you haven't taken the time to do this yet, it's not too late.

Choose your goal and record it on paper with a deadline. Then make your plan and take action every day until your goal is achieved.

You can take control your life.

DAY 176

Persistence guarantees that results are inevitable.
~Paramahansa Yogananda

Persist with your positive actions until they become habits. Persist with your positive habits and you'll achieve success. It's inevitable.

DAY 177

Successful people do what unsuccessful people are not willing to do.
~Jim Rohn

If you want to achieve success, you have to do what needs to be done. Successful people were not born special. In the beginning, it was hard for them too. But, they continued with their positive actions until their goal was achieved. The same is possible for you.

DAY 178

*Change is hardest at the beginning,
messiest in the middle and best at the end.*
~Robin S. Sharma

The journey to our goal creates the person we become: the person who can achieve their goal. Embrace the whole process. It's there for a reason.

DAY 179

*In truth, people can generally make time for what they choose
to do; it is not really the time but the will that is lacking.*
~Sir John Lubbock

Every choice you make is a decision to do one thing over another. Are you choosing to do what brings you closer to your goal?

DAY 180

You are confined only by the walls you build yourself.
~Andrew Murphy

It can be easy to build walls around ourselves, especially when we allow negative thoughts to grow in our minds. Tear down the walls and embrace your life. Every day is worth living.

DAY 181

You may be whatever you resolve to Be.
~Joel Hawes

Your past does not equal your future. With determination, you can create a whole new life. You already have the power within you. Just decide to use it.

DAY 182

Your fear is 100% dependent on you for its survival.
~Steve Maraboli

If nature fed its fears the way we do:

The tree wouldn't grow high enough
to provide refreshing shade.

The flower would never bloom
into its beautiful color.

The baby bird would never learn to fly.

Don't feed your fears.

Feed your potential instead!

DAY 183

Many things which cannot be overcome when they are together yield themselves up when taken little by little.
~Plutarch

Don't let the size of your challenge overwhelm you. Take one small step at a time. With every step you take, the next one will be revealed.

DAY 184

Why should we think upon things that are lovely? Because thinking determines life. It is a common habit to blame life upon the environment. Environment modifies life but does not govern life. The soul is stronger than its surroundings.
~William James

We are stronger than our surroundings. Claim your strength to live a powerful life. Choose victory over your circumstances.

DAY 185

*Whatever we expect with confidence
becomes our own self-fulfilling prophecy.*
~Brian Tracy

Are you hoping to find success, but expecting
to fail? It's time to expect success with your
whole mind and heart. That's when you'll
create the success you're hoping to see.

DAY 186

*It had long since come to attention that people of
accomplishment rarely sat back and let things happen to them.
They went out and happened to things.*
~Leonardo da Vinci

Make things happen in your life.
Take action every day toward your goal.

DAY 187

*Don't make excuses for why you're not doing what
you have already deemed critical to your success.*
~Lorii Myers

When you make the decision to set a goal,
you've decided that purpose is essential to
your life. When you feel the pull of old
habits, remember why you started.

DAY 188

What you do today can improve all your tomorrows.
~Ralph Marston

Today, right now, this very moment is the
time to take action. Use every precious
moment you have to move
toward your dreams.

DAY 189

Each life is made up of
mistakes and learning, waiting and growing,
practicing patience and being persistent.
~Billy Graham

Don't expect life to be perfect.
Don't think you are the only one who
has problems in the world.

To think that life shouldn't have
problems is a problem.

Know the challenges you face are all
part of the journey. The way you
choose to feel about the problems
makes the difference between a
pleasant or stressful experience.

Don't make life harder. Choose
thoughts that empower you to live life,
instead of waiting for perfection.

DAY 190

Hard work towards achieving your goals does not take something out of you. It puts something in . . . The mindset that you can achieve whatever you want to!
~Jerry Bruckner

Taking consistent daily action toward your goal creates momentum to achieve the goal. You build your confidence and self-esteem while transforming your life.

DAY 191

Good luck is another name for tenacity of purpose.
~Ralph Waldo Emerson

It's funny how some people look at others who've achieved success as being lucky. It's not about luck. It's about having a strong mind, doing the hard work, and having the will to succeed.

DAY 192

Never give up, for this is just the place and
time that the tide will turn.
~Harriet Beecher Stowe

When the journey has been long, and you feel weak, don't give up. You are so much closer to your goal than when you began. Success is closer than you know.

DAY 193

Sometimes you win, sometimes you learn.
~John Maxwell

When things don't go as planned, see that as feedback. Learn, adjust, and move forward. That makes life much more rewarding.

DAY 194

It all begins and ends in your mind. What you give power to, has power over you, if you allow it.
~Leon Brown

Are you controlling your thoughts?
Negative thinking gives your power away.
Positive thinking empowers you to achieve more.

DAY 195

Character is doing what you don't want to do but know you should do.
~Joyce Meyer

Achieving something worthwhile is never easy. Don't let your feelings keep you from doing what needs to be done.
The reward will be well worth the effort.

DAY 196

Kites rise highest against the wind, not with it.
~Winston S. Churchill

Resistance from the wind causes
a kite to soar into the sky.

The same principle applies to us.

Our resistance comes from the
challenges and obstacles we face
while working toward our goals.

Conquer those challenges
and rise to new heights.

Once you do that, your life
will never be the same.

DAY 197

Be thankful for what you have; you'll end up having more. If you concentrate on what you don't have, you will never, ever have enough.
~Oprah Winfrey

What you focus on grows. When you are thankful, you'll discover even more to be grateful for in your life. If you focus on what you lack, you'll find more lacking.

DAY 198

When any object or purpose is clearly held in thought, its precipitation, in tangible and visible form, is merely a question of time.
~Lillian Whiting

Always keep an image of your goal being achieved in your mind. Think about it day and night until that image becomes your reality.

DAY 199

Success means having the courage, the determination, and the will to become the person you believe you were meant to be.
~George Sheehan

You have the choice of remaining the same or becoming who you want to Be. Choose to Be and then take action every day until you're transformed.

DAY 200

There is a vast difference between simply thinking, and directing our thought consciously, systematically, and constructively.
~Charles Haanel

The intensity of your focus is the key to unlocking the door of success. Don't just think, take control and direct your thoughts to achieve your success.

DAY 201

*Do not anticipate trouble, or worry about what
may never happen. Keep in the sunlight.*
~Benjamin Franklin

Since what we focus on grows, it makes
no sense to entertain thoughts of possible
complications. Focus on your success;
that is more important.

DAY 202

There is no failure except in no longer trying.
~Elbert Hubbard

Never, ever give up. No matter what you
are feeling today, there will always be
brighter tomorrows. Lick your wounds if
you must. Then refocus, make
adjustments, and move forward again.

DAY 203

If you don't run your own life, somebody else will.
~John Atkinson

Are you living each day as your own?

Our lives are the sum of our choices.
Every decision has consequences,
even when we're not aware of them.

Every day, you have a choice to move
closer to your goals or do nothing and
let others have control of your day.

Don't be a bystander to your own life.

Make choices that give you the freedom
to live a fuller life.

DAY 204

Self-respect is the fruit of discipline; the sense of dignity grows with the ability to say no to oneself.
~Abraham J. Heschel

Discipline doesn't take away our choices. It gives us freedom from old behaviors and opens the door to a world of new possibilities.

DAY 205

All disappointments and failures are the result of endeavoring to think one thing and producing another.
~Genevieve Behrend

Concentrate on the one thing you want, not on a multitude of other things. With focused thought comes focused action. With focused effort, you will create your success.

DAY 206

There is no power in the universe that can help a man do a thing when he thinks he cannot do it.
~Orison Swett Marden

Visualize your success with vivid detail. A strong vision will create a firm belief in your success.

DAY 207

He that rises again quickly and continues the race is as if he had never fallen.
~Molineaux

Mistakes are inevitable. When they happen, adjust course and keep moving forward. Don't waste time berating yourself. Your time will be lost, and you'll have gained nothing in return.

DAY 208

Understanding is the secret of patience.
~Neville Goddard

Understanding that patience is necessary to achieve success will make your journey easier. Don't create unnecessary stress for yourself.

DAY 209

Think of things not as they are, but as they might be.
Don't merely dream, but create.
~Robert Collier

Don't let your current situation get in the way of your dreams. What you see beyond the horizon is calling for you. Go out and meet with your success!

DAY 210

Our past may explain why we're suffering,
but we must not use it as an excuse to stay in bondage.
~Joyce Meyer

We become free when we leave
our past regrets, sorrows, and
perceived failures behind.

They are pieces of the puzzle
we call life. Now it's time to
find the new pieces and see a
fuller picture.

Don't waste any more time on
something you can't change.

Move forward and create
what you are missing.

DAY 211

Change your thoughts and you change your world.
~Norman Vincent Peale

Our thoughts are the beginning and the end of how we deal with everything in our lives. The good news is you can change your thinking whenever you decide to.

DAY 212

With determination, the dream will be fulfilled.
~Lailah Gifty Akita

Your journey will take determination and commitment. It will require you to make changes, which you once thought were impossible. But, when your goal is achieved, the feeling will be indescribable.

DAY 213

Personal growth is not a matter of learning new information, but of unlearning old limits.
~Alan Cohen

Although learning new information is often required for our journey, it's the limits we place on ourselves that hold us back. You don't need to know everything, just get started and push your limits further.

DAY 214

Life is to be enjoyed, not endured.
~Gordon B. Hinckley

Life is about living, not just existing. Don't wish your life were better, start making it better. Stop waiting for tomorrow and begin living today.

DAY 215

Permanent results come from permanent changes. . .
~Joel Fuhrman

The changes we make to achieve success are the changes we need to maintain our success. Don't ever return to old behaviors. They'll just bring you back to the same old results.

DAY 216

As he thinks, so he is; as he continues to think, so he remains.
~James Allen

Your thoughts are the beginning of the life you create. When you continue to think in the same way, you'll continue to see the same results. To change your life, you must change how you think.

DAY 217

The secret of change is to focus all of your energy, not on fighting the old, but on building the new.
~Socrates

Don't fight against your old habits by thinking about what you're missing.

When you feel deprived, you're focusing on the wrong thoughts. You're making your journey unpleasant and more difficult.

Instead, focus on how the changes will bring you the success you desire.

That's when you'll begin to build your new life instead of fighting the old one.

DAY 218

Change might not be fast and it isn't always easy. But with time and effort, almost any habit can be reshaped.
~Charles Duhigg

With determination, any habit can be changed. To achieve success, replace your harmful habits with new productive actions. Then, continue those actions until they become your new habits.

DAY 219

You are never given a wish without also being given the power to make it true.
~Richard Bach

Where there is a desire to achieve a goal, there is an ability to succeed. Start taking steps toward your goal and the path will appear.

DAY 220

Everything is hard before it is easy.
~Johann Wolfgang von Goethe

The more we do something, the easier it becomes. Think about learning to ride a bicycle or driving a car. Don't quit when all you need is a little more practice.

DAY 221

The result will be exactly in proportion to the effort expended.
~Charles Haanel

It's a law of nature that you reap what you sow. Plant a seed, nurture the seed, and the seed will grow. If you're looking for significant results, plant a big seed, do the work, and then reap your harvest.

DAY 222

Difficulties strengthen the mind as labor does the body.
~Seneca

View your challenges and obstacles as a way of learning new things. Become adaptable to overcoming your difficulties instead of falling victim to them.

DAY 223

Learn to keep the door shut, keep out of your mind and out of your world, every element that seeks admittance with no definite helpful end in view.
~George Matthew Adams

You decide what's allowed in your world. If you desire success, don't entertain the distractions.

DAY 224

*The minute you get away from fundamentals —
whether its proper technique, work ethic or
mental preparation — the bottom can fall out of
your game, your schoolwork, your job,
whatever you're doing.*
~Michael Jordon

After you have determined your goal, it's important to stick with the fundamentals to achieve success.

1. Create a detailed vision of what your life will look like once your goal has been achieved. Visualize the image daily.
2. Take action toward reaching your goal every day.
3. Stay single-mindedly focused on your goal and don't allow distractions to interfere with your determination.
4. Look at challenges, difficulties, and mistakes as learning experiences.
5. Always keep moving forward and never, ever quit.

DAY 225

The man who is perpetually hesitating which of two things he will do first will do neither.
~William Wirt

Indecision and confusion are the enemies of success. Make prompt decisions that bring you closer to your goal. The longer you are unsure, the longer you'll stay off course.

DAY 226

If you only do what is easy, you will always remain weak.
~Joyce Meyer

Studies show that our brain connections strengthen when we learn new things. Our muscles strengthen the more we work them. It's part of nature to move beyond our comfort zones to achieve more in our lives.

DAY 227

Act now. There is never any time but now,
and there never will be any time but now.
~Wallace Wattles

We cannot change the past,
and we cannot act in the future.
Make every moment count toward
your success. Start now.

DAY 228

No excuses will lead to no regrets which will
give you no limits to your potential.
~James Gordon

Excuses and regrets walk hand in hand
down the road of struggle. Remove the
excuses and you'll remove the struggle.

DAY 229

Willpower isn't something that gets handed out to some and not to others. It is a skill you can develop through understanding and practice.
~Gillian Riley

The more you use willpower, the more willpower you'll have. Use your will to stay focused on your vision. Then you'll have all the power you need to achieve your goal.

DAY 230

People are always looking for the single magic bullet that will totally change everything. There is no single magic bullet.
~Temple Grandin

There are no secrets for transforming your life. Once you accept this, you can move forward and do what needs to be done. Only then will you achieve success.

DAY 231

We can do only what we think we can do.
We can be only what we think we can be.
We can have only what we think we can have.
What we do, what we are, what we have,
all depend upon what we think.
~Robert Collier

Our thoughts are powerful.

If we seriously don't think we can
accomplish our goals, how in the
world can we achieve them?

The real work of our journey
starts in our head.

Replace your negative programming
with new empowering thoughts and
your actions toward success
will come naturally.

Change is possible,
but you have to believe that first.

DAY 232

*Saying yes to happiness means learning to say no
to things and people that stress you out.*
~Thelma Davis

Taking care of yourself is not an option, it's a necessity. Learning to say no can be one of the best decisions you can make.

DAY 233

*What you deny or ignore, you delay.
What you accept and face, you conquer.*
~Robert Tew

It seems easy to put an uncomfortable issue off until tomorrow. But, that doesn't make the problem disappear. Conquer your challenges today. You'll have less stress and feel more productive.

DAY 234

Once you learn to quit, it becomes a habit.
~Vince Lombardi, Jr.

Repeatedly starting and stopping a new behavior creates the habit of quitting. It is much easier to start by taking small actions that you can stick with over time. Then continue to add new actions as you move forward.

DAY 235

Things which matter most must never be at the mercy of things which matter least.
~Johann Wolfgang von Goethe

Knowing your priorities is essential to achieving your goals. Don't let distractions get in the way of doing what matters most.

DAY 236

*You have a choice every day . . . you can choose every
morning whether you will be depressed and miserable,
or whether you will be happy.*
~Norman Vincent Peale

Start every morning saying,
Today is a beautiful day in every way!
Then look for beauty wherever you go.

DAY 237

Without courage, wisdom bears no fruit.
~Baltasar Gracian

All the knowledge in the world doesn't
mean anything unless it's used. When you
learn something new, apply it to your life
immediately. If you don't, there's a
possibility you never will.

DAY 238

For many people, change is more threatening than challenging.
They see it as the destroyer of what is familiar and comfortable
rather than the creator of what is new and exciting.
~Nido R. Qubein

Change can be scary for people who
haven't left their comfort zone in a while.

Even though they're unhappy where
they are, they refuse to do anything
to disrupt their routines.

When you become the cause of change,
your life becomes new and exciting.

Don't be comfortable and complacent.
Push your boundaries; there is so much
more to experience.

DAY 239

If you don't think you can do it, who will?
You control the most important tool in success, your mind.
~Jeffrey Gitomer

Don't rely on others for your success. No one can have more of an impact on your journey than you can.

DAY 240

We are a product of the choices we make,
not the circumstances that we face.
~Roger Crawford

We will have both good days and not so good days during our journey. Don't let difficulties deflect you from your goal. Use the challenges to learn, adjust, grow stronger, and move ahead.

DAY 241

If your compassion does not include yourself, it is incomplete.
~Jack Kornfield

We can be one of our harshest critics. But, we should be our biggest cheerleader. It is much easier to achieve a goal when you're there to support yourself.

DAY 242

If not now, when?
~Hillel the Elder

If you wait for the perfect time to begin moving toward your goal, you'll be waiting a long time. The best time to get started is always right now.

DAY 243

Doing the best at this moment puts you in the best place for the next moment.
~Oprah Winfrey

Every step we take prepares us for the next. If you are not doing your best now, it will be harder to do better later. You'll get farther faster when you build momentum by doing the best you can with every action to take.

DAY 244

Aerodynamically, the bumble bee shouldn't be able to fly, but the bumble bee doesn't know it so it goes on flying anyway.
~Mary Kay Ash

Sometimes knowing too much can become intimidating. You don't need to know every detail to start. Just get started with what you know now.

DAY 245

Real motivation is that drive from within:
You know where you are going because you have a compelling
image inside, not on a travel poster on the wall.
~Denis Waitley

Nothing from outside yourself can motivate you more than the inner flame of determination.

To ignite your internal motivation, begin by visualizing your goal as achieved with vivid detail.

Then focus on that image day and night until you feel like the person you desire to be.

That's when you'll feel the drive to transform your vision into reality.

That's when you'll feel real motivation.

DAY 246

Act the way you'd like to be, and soon you'll be the way you act.
~Leonard Cohen

When you take on the characteristics
of the person you want to Be,
it won't be long until you
become that person.

DAY 247

At any given moment, you have the power to say:
This is not how the story is going to end.
~Christine Mason

You've prepared your whole life for this
moment. Now it's time to change your
story. What will you do differently today?

DAY 248

Show up in every single moment like you're meant to be there.
~Marie Forleo

It is your time to BE right now.
Don't keep waiting for tomorrow.
BE strong, BE confident, BE amazing. BE
your authentic self today.

DAY 249

One part at a time, one day at a time,
we can accomplish any goal we set for ourselves.
~Karen Casey

Don't overwhelm yourself.
Breaking your goal down into smaller
pieces is the easiest way to achieve success.

DAY 250

There are no failures -
just experiences and your reactions to them.
~Tom Krause

Failure is such a harsh word. Remove it from your vocabulary. Look at every challenge as a new learning experience. That's all it really is.

DAY 251

Change is not a process for the impatient.
~Barbara Reinhold

Reaching your goal may take longer than you'd like. Don't let that stop you from doing what needs to be done. As long as you never quit, your success is inevitable.

DAY 252

*If you are not in the process of becoming
the person you want to be, you are automatically
engaged in becoming the person you don't want to be.*
~Dale Carnegie

Every day we face an array of decisions.

Some decisions are more significant
and others are much smaller. And then,
there are the decisions we avoid.

We think if a decision hasn't been made,
it doesn't' matter.

However, those indecisions are a choice
too. By not deciding, we've automatically
chosen not to do something.

And, that choice keeps us with the
same old results we've always had.

DAY 253

People with goals succeed because they know where they're going.
~Earl Nightingale

Without a goal to move toward, we are like a boat on the water without a rudder. The circumstances in our lives are like the waves that push the boat back and forth with no direction. Having a goal gives you a destination. Then you can navigate the circumstances, instead of having them push you.

DAY 254

Forget past mistakes and forget failures.
Forget everything except what you are going to do now and do it.
~William J. Durant

To move forward, you can't live in the past. You've already paid the penalty for past regrets. Step forward and begin to create something new.

DAY 255

Always imagine and expect the best.
~Neville Goddard

Too often, people use their imagination to picture all the reasons why they can't do something. Don't waste your energy expecting the worst. What you focus on grows. Picture all the reasons why you can.

DAY 256

The only way to keep from going backward is to keep moving forward.
~Charles Haanel

Standing still in life is not an option, especially if you are not happy where you are. You can create change, just take that first step forward.

DAY 257

Self-discipline is self-caring.
~M. Scott Peck

Self-discipline is not punishment. It's a way to remove unwanted habits from your life. The old habits were made unconsciously. Self-discipline is the way you consciously choose new habits. Change your habits and you change your life.

DAY 258

A successful person is just a novice who started and kept on going.
~Maddy Malhotra

Sometimes we look at successful people like they have something special. What they have is a spirit of never quitting. No matter how hard their journey was, they stayed on course until their goal was achieved.

DAY 259

When obstacles arise, you change your direction to reach your goal; you do not change your decision to get there.
~Zig Ziglar

Sometimes our best-laid plans are forced off track by unexpected events.

But, that doesn't mean we should give up on ourselves or our goals.

Be wise with your decisions and your time, especially when dealing with people or situations that are outside your control.

Protect your dream.
It's there for a reason.

DAY 260

Life can only be understood backwards;
but it must be lived forwards.
~Soren Kierkegaard

We don't always know why challenges arise in our lives. But, often with time, we see the meaning later. Use a challenge to increase your knowledge and strength, instead of it being an overwhelming burden.

DAY 261

Doing what needs to be done may not make you happy,
but it will make you great.
~George Bernard Shaw

We may not always feel like doing what needs to be done. But, overcoming those feelings is what sets apart those who succeed from those who do not.

DAY 262

You have been criticizing yourself for years and it hasn't worked. Try approving of yourself and see what happens.
~Louise Hay

To achieve our goals, we need to believe that we are worthy and capable. If you don't think you can reach your goal, let that be the first thing you work on changing.

DAY 263

*Worrying is like a rocking chair,
it gives you something to do, but it gets you nowhere.*
~Glenn Turner

The only thing worrying does
is to keep you from focusing
on what really matters.

DAY 264

Winners compare their achievements with their goals, while losers compare their achievements with those of other people.
~Nido R. Qubein

Comparing yourself to others is the surest way of causing yourself stress. Instead, focus on how far you've come since beginning your journey. That's all that really matters.

DAY 265

You may encounter many defeats, but you must not be defeated. In fact, it may be necessary to encounter the defeats, so you can know who you are, what you can rise from, how you can still come out of it.
~Maya Angelou

The obstacles we face while reaching our goal are the lessons we learn to achieve our goal.

DAY 266

It is better to take many small steps in the right direction than to make a great leap forward only to stumble backward.
~Louis Sachar

Sometimes when people get a taste of motivation, their first impulse is to take a super-sized action in a very short time-frame.

When that happens, they quickly discover what can't be done.
Then, they begin to question their goals, and their motivation wanes during the process.

Don't set yourself up for failure.

Start with small steps that can be accomplished. Build your confidence for something bigger and your motivation will increase. That sets you up for success.

DAY 267

Nothing can stop the man with the right mental attitude from achieving his goal; nothing on earth can help the man with the wrong mental attitude.
~Thomas Jefferson

Thinking negatively about your life will never allow you to have a successful experience. Having a positive attitude opens the door to unimagined possibilities.

DAY 268

Gratitude is the law of increase, and complaint is the law of decrease.
~Florence Scovel Shinn

Being thankful automatically connects you to the positive mindset of increase. How much easier can it be?

DAY 269

Dripping water hollows out stone,
not through force but through persistence.
~Ovid

Persistence guarantees your success. It's the spirit of never giving up. Without persistence, you only have a wish.

DAY 270

All you need is to know what you want,
and to want it badly enough so it will stay in your thoughts.
~Wallace Wattles

Simply fall in love with your goal. When you're in love, it doesn't take any effort to keep the image in your thoughts.

DAY 271

Concentrate on the things you want, not things you don't want.
~Charles Haanel

What you think about grows. If your mind is
concentrating on what you don't want in your
life, you will see more of those situations.
Instead, focus on the things you do want
in your life. Then better circumstances
will begin to bloom.

DAY 272

It's not that some people have willpower and some don't.
It's that some people are ready to change and others are not.
~James Gordon

Change happens when the pain
of staying where you are is stronger
than the pain it takes to make the change.

DAY 273

Problems cannot be solved by the same
level of thinking that created them.
~Albert Einstein

Making a change in life without
changing your thinking is like
painting over a water stain
without fixing the leak.

It will look nice for a moment, but the
stain will return because its cause was
never repaired. The only way to
permanently remove the stain
is to fix the leak first.

To make permanent changes in your
life, you need to repair the cause of
your circumstances. That happens by
changing how you think first.

DAY 274

*High achievement always takes place
in the framework of high expectation.*
~Charles Kettering

If you already have expectations for your
life, why settle for mediocre when you can
have so much more?

DAY 275

*Whenever inner speech and desire are in conflict,
inner speech invariably wins.*
~Neville Goddard

Pay attention to that little voice inside.
If it isn't lining up with what you plan
to achieve, it will keep you from
reaching your goal.

DAY 276

The first step toward success is taken when you refuse to be captive of the environment in which you first find yourself.
~Mark Caine

Being unhappy with your current
circumstances is the first sign
that you're ready for a change.
Take a step forward and break free.

DAY 277

Avoid negative people at all costs.
They are the greatest destroyers of self-confidence and self-esteem.
~Brian Tracy

Negative people love drama. They're drawn to
drama. When they can't find drama, they'll
create their own. There's no room for drama
lovers when you're reaching for your goal.

DAY 278

Shallow men believe in luck.
Strong men believe in cause and effect.
~Ralph Waldo Emerson

Every decision has consequences. Your choices are the cause that effects the results you see in your life.

DAY 279

If I really want to improve my situation, I can work on the one thing over which I have control — myself.
~Stephen Covey

There are so many things that are out of our control. For real change to occur in our lives, the change must begin within ourselves.

DAY 280

*Many people fail in life, not for lack of ability or brains
or even courage but simply because they have never
organized their energies around a goal.*
~Elbert Hubbard

Having a goal gives your actions meaning.

People rush around all day long,
but not everyone takes the right
actions toward a goal.

They flutter around all day and are
exhausted by nightfall without
accomplishing anything significant.

Don't spend your energy on things
that do not matter.

Accomplish great things by acting
on what's important first.

DAY 281

The grass is greener where you water it.
~Neil Barringham

Nurture your dream daily by taking
action and visualizing your goal
as being achieved.

DAY 282

If you can't fly then run, if you can't run then walk,
if you can't walk then crawl, but whatever you do
you have to keep moving forward.
~Martin Luther King, Jr.

Wherever you are, with whatever you have,
start now. The rest will come with time. You
build your future with every step forward.

DAY 283

If you learn from a loss you have not lost.
~Austin O'Malley

Carry no regrets for the things that
have made you who you are.
Move forward and create
something new from the
lessons you have learned.

🦋🦋🦋🦋

DAY 284

Better to do something imperfectly than to do nothing flawlessly.
~Robert Schuller

Don't wait until you can do
something perfectly. Begin now
and look for progress. Doing nothing
isn't an option for creating success.

DAY 285

All progress takes place outside the comfort zone.
~Michael John Bobak

Once you step out of your comfort
zone, you begin to live life
in a whole new beautiful way.

DAY 286

Small deeds done are better than great deeds planned.
~Peter Marshall

We can make plans, review our plans,
and adjust our plans. But, until we
take action, nothing happens.

DAY 287

Through discipline comes freedom.
~Aristotle

Real freedom comes from having choices.

When you are held captive to a
harmful habit, you have no control.
The habit is controlling you.

Discipline allows you to take
back your control.

Once you're in control, you'll have
the ability to make choices again.

When you replace a harmful habit with a
new positive habit, you'll experience the
freedom you've longed to have.

DAY 288

Stand up to your obstacles and do something about them. You'll find they haven't half the strength you think they have.
~Norman Vincent Peale

You are stronger than you think. Don't give power to your challenges. Tackle them quickly and move on.

DAY 289

The strongest people aren't always the people who win, but the people who don't give up when they lose.
~Ashley Hodgeson

Your strength grows with every circumstance you overcome. And, often you learn more from losing than if you had won.

DAY 290

You are the designer of your destiny;
you are the author of your story.
~Lisa Nichols

When you have a vision for your life, you're creating your story. If you live each day as it comes, with no direction, you're allowing others to write the story for you.

✖ ✖ ✖ ✖

DAY 291

Do, every day, all that you can do that day,
and do each action in an efficient manner.
~Wallace Wattles

Apply your best effort to everything you do. When you do, you'll soon become the person you wish to Be.

DAY 292

It is feeling that imparts vitality to thought.
~Charles Haanel

When you mix the feelings of accomplishment with thoughts about your goal, it's a combination that ignites the spark of success.

DAY 293

There are two types of people who will tell you that you cannot make a difference in this world: those who are afraid to try and those who are afraid you will succeed.
~Ray Goforth

Don't listen to naysayers. You never know what their real motives are.

DAY 294

You don't have to see the whole staircase,
just take the first step.
~Martin Luther King, Jr.

We usually don't know all the details
of our journey in advance. But, we
still need to take that first step, and
all the other steps in between there
and our destination.

It's like climbing a set of stairs,
not knowing what's at the top.
We do that every day without
ever thinking about it.

Decide what your next step is
and then just take it.

DAY 295

It's sometimes easier to help others rather than helping yourself.
The trick is to listen to your "self" as a friend.
This may be the simplest change you ever make in life,
with the biggest impact.
~Lorii Myers

Care for yourself as much as you do for others in
your life. When you do this, you are caring for
both yourself and those you love.

DAY 296

It is quite unfortunate that some of the thoughts that the mind
produces can turn around and reward it with a lifetime of pain
and suffering. But fortunately, positive thoughts have never
failed to deliver happiness to any mind that shelters them.
~Edmond Mbiaka

Don't choke the life out of your dreams with
negative thinking. Feed your dreams with
positive expectations.

DAY 297

If you decide to just go with the flow, you'll end up where the flow goes, which is usually downhill, often leading to a big pile of sludge and a life of unhappiness.
~Sean Covey

By taking control of your thoughts, actions, and habits, every area of your life will improve. Don't go with the flow; turn the current to your favor.

DAY 298

Don't lose faith. Promise yourself that you will be a success story, and I promise you that all the forces of the universe will unite to come to your aid; you might not feel it today or for a while, but the longer you wait the bigger the prize.
~George Bernard Shaw

There is no secret to success. You do what needs to be done and keep doing that until you reach your goal.

DAY 299

Life's inevitable changes are like a compulsory roller-coaster ride. You can cower and shut your eyes tight, or you can exult in the thrills.
~Roger Crawford

Everything we see in life is affected by our perceptions. Change how you feel about something and you'll change everything about it.

DAY 300

A man is but the product of his thoughts — what he thinks, he becomes.
~Mohandas Gandhi

The way you think about yourself determines your behaviors. Your behaviors create the life you live. If you're not happy with your circumstances, it's time to change the way you're thinking.

DAY 301

If you believe you can, you probably can. If you believe you won't, you most assuredly won't. Belief is the ignition switch that gets you off the launching pad.
~Denis Waitley

Erase all doubt from your mind.

Visualize yourself living with
your goal already being achieved.
And then, build that image with
vivid details until it consumes
your thoughts.

When you become that focused
on your goal, nothing will stop
you from reaching it.

DAY 302

Victory is not won in miles but in inches. Win a little now, hold your ground, and later win a little more.
~Louis L'Amour

Every step you take moving forward gets you closer to your goal. It doesn't matter how big of a step you take. Just keep stepping forward.

DAY 303

A nail is driven out by another nail; habit is overcome by habit.
~Desiderius Erasmus

It's much easier to replace a negative habit with new positive habit than it is to just stop doing the negative habit alone.

DAY 304

Without self-discipline, success is impossible, period.
~Lou Holtz

Different results require different behaviors. We can't continue with the same actions and expect a change in the outcome.

DAY 305

It is frequent repetition that produces a natural tendency.
~Aristotle

We create a habit by consistently repeating a specific behavior. Over time that habit becomes part of our routine and no thought is needed to complete the action. Create positive habits to build a routine that takes you to your goal.

DAY 306

*Blaming our behavior on forces outside ourselves
is a way of avoiding responsibility.*
~James Redfield

Accept responsibility for your thoughts,
actions, and results. When you do, you'll
gain control over your circumstances.

DAY 307

Men stumble over pebbles, never over mountains.
~H. Emilie Cady

Small things can make a big difference
in our results. Don't let the size of an
action mislead you into thinking it's
too little to matter.

183

DAY 308

The season of failure is the best time for
sowing the seeds of success.
~Paramahansa Yogananda

It's easy to let a setback pull us off track.

Instead of taking a deep dive
into despair, use your will to focus
on your goal as being achieved. See it,
feel it, and believe it.

Then you won't be feeding the
weeds in your mind.

You'll be nurturing the seeds
of your success.

DAY 309

The trick is to enjoy life. Don't wish away your days, waiting for better ones ahead.
~Marjorie Pay Hinckley

Today is a gift. Don't waste it on circumstances you cannot change. Instead, be thankful for all the beauty that surrounds you.

DAY 310

It is never too late to be what you might have been.
~George Eliot

As long as we're breathing, we can have hope. Change is only a step forward in a new direction. You can become everything that you ever wanted to Be. Start now and begin your transformation.

DAY 311

Permanence, perseverance and persistence in spite of all obstacles, discouragements, and impossibilities: It is this, that in all things distinguishes the strong soul from the weak.
~Thomas Carlyle

It's not always going to be easy.
But, if you do what needs to be done,
your harvest will be bountiful.

DAY 312

It can be done and you are the one to do it.
~David V. Bush

The vision you have of your goal achieved
is there because you can do it. It's all yours
if you're willing to make it happen.

DAY 313

A bend in the road is not the end of the road . . . unless you fail to make the turn.
~Helen Keller

Having plans to reach your goal is a great way to stay focused. But, be prepared for unexpected events. Sometimes we need to change the plans, but never the focus.

DAY 314

The will is your most important asset. If you lose it, you have lost everything.
~Dele Ayo Bankole

The more you use your will, the stronger it grows. When you are willing to make a change, you will find the way.

DAY 315

I think that we are like stars.
Something happens to burst us open;
but when we burst open and think we are dying;
we're actually turning into a supernova.
And then when we look at ourselves again,
we see that we're suddenly more beautiful
than we ever were before.
~C. JoyBell C.

We don't always know the reasons
why something stressful happens
in our lives.

And, sometimes the pain seems
more than we can bear.

But, in your darkest hours,
don't give up.

You will become more from this
challenging time. You will be
more beautiful in every way.

DAY 316

*Magic is believing in yourself, if you can do that,
you can make anything happen.*
~Johann Wolfgang von Goethe

The power to change your life is already
within you. But, you have to believe that
you can become the person you want Be.
Your possibilities are limitless, once you
accept who you are.

DAY 317

*Waste your money and you're only out of money, but waste your
time and you've lost a part of your life.*
~Michael LeBoeuf

Our time is more precious than jewels.
Don't waste your days like
they're pennies.

DAY 318

*Let the power of yes take root in your heart
and transform your life.*
~Bryant McGill

Yes, I can!
Say it, feel it, and believe it.

DAY 319

*Wishes and wants do not transform a person; actions and
reactions do so! Show the world your plans by the actions you
take progressively and consistently.*
~Israelmore Ayivor

Stay focused on the actions that bring you
closer to your goal. If you are not doing what
needs to be done, you are not doing
anything about getting there.

DAY 320

Change happens for you the moment you want
something more than you fear it.
~Eric Micha'el Leventhal

Build your dreams with vivid details,
until your fears have dissolved.

DAY 321

You have power over your mind – not outside events.
Realize this, and you will find strength.
~Marcus Aurelius

It's not complicated. Focus on what you
can control. Change your thoughts and
you'll change your actions, which will
change your life.

DAY 322

Each person has got a voice inside them.
Communicate with it and take hold of it.
Do not let it push and shove you around.
~Stephen Richards

The capabilities of our self-talk
are astounding.

Yet, so few people consciously
choose to use this creative ability.

Instead, we let our self-talk rob us
of achieving our dreams,
with negative and critical chatter.

Take control of your self-talk
and that incredible power
will become your ally instead
of your foe.

DAY 323

Worry does not empty tomorrow of its sorrow,
it empties today of its strength.
~Corrie ten Boom

Worrying keeps you busy with thoughts
that provide no value to your life. Break
free from worrying and think of things as
you would like them to be instead.

DAY 324

Your problem is you're... too busy
holding onto your unworthiness.
~Ram Dass

Forgive yourself for past regrets and embrace
who you are today. Loving yourself allows you
to take care of yourself. When you appreciate
who you are, you'll finally Be who you've
always wanted to become.

DAY 325

It is good to have an end to journey toward;
but it is the journey that matters, in the end.
~Ursula K. Le Guin

The journey toward our goal is where we learn how to become successful. Appreciate every moment, and value all the lessons along the way.

DAY 326

You must give everything to make your life as beautiful
as the dreams that dance in your imagination.
~Roman Payne

You have an opportunity every day to create a beautiful life. Don't let circumstances stand in your way. Do whatever needs to be done to bring your dreams to life.

DAY 327

Don't wait for things to happen. Make them happen.
~Roy Bennett

Don't waste your time waiting for someday. You have the power to change at this very moment.
Go and make something happen!

🦋🦋🦋🦋

DAY 328

If you don't take the time to get really clear about exactly what it is you're trying to accomplish, then you're forever doomed to spend your life achieving the goals of those who do.
~Steve Pavlina

It's not enough to have a vague idea of what you want in your life. You must want it with all your heart. When you want something that much, your vision will become intensely clear.

DAY 329

Inaction breeds doubt and fear.
Action breeds confidence and courage.
If you want to conquer fear,
do not sit home and think about it.
Go out and get busy.
~Dale Carnegie

Confidence and courage grow with use.

Start by setting smaller goals
that you can quickly achieve
to build your confidence.

After every achievement, make the
next short-term goal a little bigger.

Keep repeating this process until
your confidence is so high that
nothing seems impossible.

DAY 330

Believe in your dreams. They were given to you for a reason.
~Katrina Mayer

Your dreams are a special gift.
When you transform them into reality,
you share your gift with the world.

DAY 331

Don't let reality get in the way of your dreams.
~Anthony Liccione

Don't let the situations in your life hold
you back. What you desire will make you
stronger than any challenge you'll face.

DAY 332

I have found that if you love life, life will love you back.
~Arthur Rubinstein

The way you perceive your life is the way you'll experience your life.

✖✖✖✖

DAY 333

As soon as you trust yourself, you will know how to live.
~Johann Wolfgang von Goethe

One of the best parts of working toward a goal is getting to know and trust yourself. The more you feel like your authentic self, the better your life becomes.

DAY 334

Our greatest weakness lies in giving up. The most certain way to succeed is always to try just one more time.
~Thomas A. Edison

If you never give up,
your success is inevitable!

DAY 335

Don't let people who don't care about you manipulate your mind, feelings and emotions or control how you think about yourself. Never give that much power to someone else.
~Karon Waddell

Every time you give your control away, you lose pieces of yourself. Reclaim your power and take your life back. You are much stronger than you think.

DAY 336

You'll never cross an emotional bridge,
if you keep rushing back to the other side.
~T.F. Hodge

We often think that reliving our past will allow us to move on from our regrets and sorrows. That is fine if we find healing.

But, when we become a hostage of those events, we lose our current days of living life.

Stop reliving the past and focus on creating your future.

You have the key to the freedom you seek.

Accept your past for what it was, but move forward and begin to rebuild the life you have today.

DAY 337

It is not your passing thoughts or brilliant ideas so much as your plain everyday habits that control your life.
~Paramahansa Yogananda

Our daily behaviors create the life we experience. If you are not happy with your results, replace the habits that are causing your predicament.

DAY 338

Work without vision is drudgery. Vision without work is dreaming. Work plus vision – this is destiny.
~Gordon B. Hinckley

Working on someone else's dream feels like drudgery. Instead, start working on your dream. It doesn't matter how big of a step you take. Begin to create your destiny today.

DAY 339

Your intellect may be confused,
but your emotions will never lie to you.
~Roger Ebert

The way we feel gives us an indication of the
thoughts we are thinking. When we feel
stressed, fearful, and sad, we're having
negative thoughts. Feelings of well-being
are always the result of positive thinking.

DAY 340

There are two primary choices in life: to accept conditions as
they exist, or accept the responsibility for changing them.
~Denis Waitley

Many meaningful days are wasted by not
taking responsibility for the life we live.
Don't blame; begin creating the life you'd
rather be living.

DAY 341

Clouds come floating into my life, no longer to carry rain
or usher storm, but to add color to my sunset sky.
~Rabindranath Tagore

Our life is a reflection of the way we
choose to think. After it rains, we can
see the rainbow or decide to look
for mud puddles.

DAY 342

Life's blows cannot break a person whose spirit
is warmed by the fire of enthusiasm.
~Norman Vincent Peale

When you have a passion for your goal,
you'll look beyond obstacles and challenges
for a solution. Passion gives you the energy
to overcome the challenges instead of
being defeated by them.

DAY 343

Nobody can go back and start a new beginning,
but anyone can start today and make a new ending.
~Maria Robinson

Have you decided to make a
new ending for yourself?

Our past shapes who we are,
but it doesn't define who
we can become.

What you do today will shape
who you become tomorrow.

Believe in yourself no matter
where you've been. You can
reshape your future.

Start today!

DAY 344

Adopt the pace of nature: her secret is patience.
~Ralph Waldo Emerson

Everything takes time in nature. Our world of instant downloads has not prepared us to wait patiently for our success. Do what needs to be done every day. The reward will appear at the proper time. That's how nature works.

DAY 345

We have more control than most of us realize.
Each day is filled with thousands of opportunities
to change the story of our lives.
~Michael Hyatt

Don't accept what life is handing out. Instead, choose to create the life you desire. When you know what you want, you will see new opportunities when they appear.

DAY 346

Success doesn't come to you, you go to it.
~Marva Collins

Every decisive action you take
toward your goal brings you closer
to discovering your success.

✖✖✖✖

DAY 347

*Failure will never overtake me if my determination
to succeed is strong enough.*
~Og Mandino

Failure isn't even an option
when you are fully committed and
determined to reach your goal.

DAY 348

A large oak tree is just a little nut that refused to give up.
~David McGee

When we look at nature, we can see the unfolding of beauty every day. Now, realize that you have more power than an acorn. Imagine the possibilities waiting for you to become what you're meant to Be.

DAY 349

You are very powerful,
provided you know how powerful you are.
~Yogi Bhajan

People who harness their power achieve what others only hope to. Yet, we all have the same power available. Some people choose to accept it, and others don't even realize it's there.

DAY 350

Discipline is the bridge between goals and accomplishment.
~Jim Rohn

We usually look at the word
"discipline" like it means deprivation.
But, the truth is, we need to use
discipline to reach our goals.

Discipline gives us the freedom
to live a fuller life.

Change the way you feel
about the word discipline and
you'll change the way you live.

Don't perceive discipline as a
negative; instead, look at it as
the bridge that leads to a
brighter future.

DAY 351

What a caterpillar calls the end
of the world we call a butterfly.
~Eckhart Tolle

The process of transformation is not painless. The transition takes time. If we quit during the process, we'll never see the beauty that waits on the other side.

DAY 352

Gratitude magnifies the sweet parts of life
and diminishes the painful ones.
~Yuval Levin

Take a moment and reflect on the "sweet parts" of your life. No matter where you are on this journey, there is something to be thankful for today.

DAY 353

Life is not a problem to be solved,
but a reality to be experienced.
~Soren Kierkegaard

Life is about LIVING.

✕✕✕✕

DAY 354

Live out of your imagination instead of your memory.
~Les Brown

When we let go of the past, we permit
ourselves to create a new future. Take the
lessons you have learned and create
something extraordinary with your life.

DAY 355

Intuition is seeing with the soul.
~Dean Koontz

When in doubt, always follow your intuition. Don't over think a situation, just follow your gut feeling. It will guide you in the right direction.

DAY 356

Every tomorrow is determined by every today.
~Paramahansa Yogananda

Do something today that will help you create a better tomorrow.

DAY 357

Affirmations are our mental vitamins, providing the supplementary positive thoughts we need to balance the barrage of negative events and thoughts we experience daily.
~Tia Walker

Using a powerful affirmation consistently helps to build a positive resistance to all the negativity that surrounds us.

Make a short, concise, and easy to remember statement for yourself.

Say it when you wake up, say it mid-day, and say it before falling asleep. And, repeat it anytime you have negative thoughts throughout the day.

The more you say your affirmation, the stronger you will become.

Here is an example you can use:
I am worthy, deserving, powerful, capable, and confident.

DAY 358

Coasting only takes you downhill.
~Roger Crawford

Moving forward is a necessity for living a successful life. Always have a dream and a purpose to pursue. It will make living a magical experience.

DAY 359

Reality is created by the mind;
we can change our reality by changing our mind.
~Plato

The power to change is always available. Just concentrate on what you want the most. That sets everything else into motion. This principle works whether you believe it or not. Look at what you're currently thinking about, and then notice the circumstances in your life today.

DAY 360

There is a great difference between a need and a desire.
~Claude M. Bristol

Having a desire is what adds the spark of enthusiasm to achieving your goal. Wanting something new to experience is what makes a goal an exciting adventure to pursue. When you have that all-encompassing focus you'll truly achieve success.

DAY 361

A mood, often repeated, gains a momentum that is hard to break or check. So be careful of the feelings you entertain.
~Neville Goddard

The principal of momentum works for both negative and positive results. Your feelings will give you an indication of where your mind is focusing. Make sure it's where you want to be going.

DAY 362

*You are going to be successful because you are going to do
two things. You're going to learn new things,
and then you are going to do them.*
~T. Harv Eker

Learn what you need to accomplish your
goal. Then apply what you learn to your
life. Both are required to succeed.

DAY 363

If you want to be happy, be!
~Henry David Thoreau

Be who you were meant to Be.
Be everything you desire to Be.
Be who you authentically are.

DAY 364

Don't expect life to get easier but be prepared to get stronger.
~Karon Waddell

A change in perspective changes how we react to the circumstances of our life.

If we expect life to become easier, we are setting ourselves up for disappointment and discouragement.

However, if we know that there will be challenges, but by overcoming them, we'll become stronger, we're setting ourselves up for success.

Instead of being overwhelmed by our challenges, we find solutions to overcome them. A small change in how you think can create significant results in your life.

DAY 365

Life is a journey of learning and adapting.
~Beth Bianca

Life can be a grand adventure or
a series of regrets.

The way we think and the way
we perceive life are within
our control.

I have chosen to see wonders and
experience the indescribable.

Will you join me?

ABOUT THE AUTHOR

Beth Bianca is the author of four books, a certified life coach and the founder of LadiesInWeighting.com. Her articles have appeared in the Huffington Post and ObesityHelp.com.

Once weighing 394 pounds, Beth was close to death when her doctor recommended weight-loss surgery. She quickly discovered that surgery was not the "easy way out" that so many people believe it to be. Beth realized, to save her life, she would have to change everything she ever thought about food.

Armed with a change in the way she perceived her journey to become healthy again, Beth lost a total of 229 pounds. Now she is passionate about helping others learn how they can change their mindset and create a new life for themselves.

Meet and connect with Beth at the following links:
Website: http://BethBianca.com/
Blog: http://LadiesInWeighting.com/
Facebook: https://www.facebook.com/BethBianca.Author/

Receive notifications of new releases and special offers.
Text the word **LIVING** to **444999**

ALSO BY BETH BIANCA

Mindset Breakthrough: *Achieve Weight-Loss Surgery Success*

The Breakthrough Journal: *Butterfly Edition*

The Breakthrough Journal: *Flower Edition*

Visit the Breakthrough Butterfly Warrior Shop
T-Shirts, Hoodies, Mugs, and More
BethBianca.com/shop/

93614013R00123

Made in the USA
Lexington, KY
16 July 2018